Acknowledgments

First and foremost, I offer my deepest thanks to my wife. Your unwavering support, patience, and belief in me have been the foundation beneath every word of this book. Through long nights, early mornings, and countless weekends sacrificed to screens and spreadsheets, you stood by me—not just with encouragement, but with grace, humour, and quiet strength. This work could not have taken shape without the space you gave me to focus, reflect, and create.

To my children — you are my greatest inspiration. Your curiosity, laughter, and boundless energy reminded me every day why we build, why we strive, and why every effort must count. I hope this book, in some small way, shows you what's possible when passion is paired with persistence.

This book is dedicated not just to the industry I've grown in, but to the family who has always been my true foundation.

Author: Tauheed Jan

Published - 2025

Book Information
Title: Numbers That Build: Mastering the Business of Estimation, Tendering, and Control in Modern Construction
Publisher: Tauheed Jan

Publication Date: 01-08-2025

ISBN: 978-93-343-7175-8

Edition: First

Description: An in-depth, story-driven guide to mastering estimation, tendering, and project control in modern construction, blending global industry best practices with practical frameworks, real-world case studies, and future-focused insights for professionals and leaders.

Target Audience:

- Mid- to senior-level professionals in construction, cost engineering, and project controls
- MBA and graduate engineering students in project management
- Project owners, consultants, government tender committees

Connect with the author: www.tauheedjan.com/contact for feedback or collaborations: contact@tauheedjan.com

About the Author

Tauheed Jan is a Project Controls Manager and EPC strategist with over 14 years of hands-on experience delivering high-value industrial and infrastructure projects across Saudi Arabia and India. With a portfolio exceeding USD 2 billion, he has held leadership roles in estimation, planning, and controls on some of the region's most complex developments—including the **Fadhili Gas Program**, **Tanajib Gas Plant**, and the **Saudi Elastomers Project**—serving clients such as **Aramco, SABIC, Técnicas Reunidas, Wison Engineering, Hyundai, etc**.

Tauheed's expertise lies in bridging planning with real-world execution. From leading corporate tendering functions that secured over USD 1.5 billion in new projects, to architecting PMO frameworks that improved reporting accuracy by over 20%, he brings a systems-level view to the construction lifecycle. His toolkit includes advanced command of **Primavera P6**, **Power BI**, **SAP**, **Oracle ERP**, and modern EVM techniques—tools he's used to consistently deliver on schedule, cost, and risk targets.

Certified as a **Project Management Professional (PMP®)** and **Lean Six Sigma Green Belt**, Tauheed combines field-tested engineering judgment with strategic business acumen. He holds a **Bachelor's in Civil Engineering** and an **MBA in Operations Management**, and is an accredited member of PMI and the Saudi Council of Engineers.

Numbers That Build reflects his long-held belief that accurate planning, transparent controls, and disciplined estimation aren't just technical exercises—they are the building blocks of trust, performance, and long-term project success.

Table of Contents

Introduction

The Numbers Behind the Skyline

Picture a windswept site outside Riyadh: the afternoon heat shimmers above a vast metro extension. Two rival bid teams—one seasoned, one ambitious—await their fate as envelopes are opened. The lower bid, dazzling on paper, is rejected after a single question exposes its flawed escalation logic. The project goes to the team whose estimate isn't the cheapest—but is the most robust.

This moment, a blend of calculation, insight, and judgment, captures the power and peril of numbers in construction.

My journey in project controls has spanned over a decade across high-impact projects in Saudi Arabia and India, from Aramco's energy mega-programs to Ministry of Defence infrastructure works. Along the way, I've learned that numbers do not just secure contracts—they shape cities and careers. I've also learned that project control isn't just about charts and dates—it's about creating clarity and momentum through structure, visibility, and early anticipation. Yet, the construction sector's reputation has been tarnished by overruns, litigation, and cultural resistance to change.

There exists a gap in both literature and practice: a need for a book that does not separate the science of estimation from the art of winning work, building trust, and adapting to future shocks. *Numbers That Build* fills that void, bringing together timeless principles, modern analytics, and real stories. It is a reference for seasoned professionals and newcomers alike, rooted in global best practice and practical frameworks you can use immediately.

Part I: Foundations

Chapter 1

The Missing Multiplier—Why Accuracy Pays Exponential Dividends

In global construction, accuracy is not just a virtue—it's a financial imperative. A small error at the project's genesis often echoes through every phase, growing exponentially and shaping project outcomes, careers, and corporate legacies. This chapter examines why minute misjudgements in estimation amplify so dramatically, drawing on data, field stories, and frameworks from the world's most ambitious projects.

1.1 Our Industry's Productivity Crisis

Despite being one of the world's largest sectors, generating over $13 trillion annually, construction productivity has lagged far behind fields like manufacturing and IT. From 2000 to 2020, construction's productivity grew at an average annual rate of less than 1%, far below the 2–3% seen in the broader economy. Several studies, including those from McKinsey and the World Economic Forum, pinpoint inaccurate early estimates and weak controls as root causes for these chronic cost overruns and delays. The "missing multiplier" is not just technology—it's the compound effect of these early-stage estimation errors.

Key Data Points:

- **McKinsey Global Institute:** 98% of megaprojects experience cost or schedule overruns.
- **PwC Global Construction Survey:** Over 60% of projects cite poor early-stage estimation as the reason for major budget variation.

Visualization: Icon Array
(Represents 100 megaprojects)

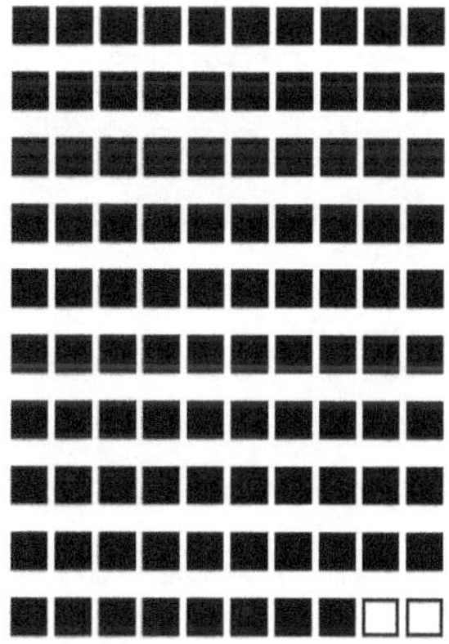

Key:

- ■ = Project with Overrun (98%)
- □ = Project On-Time / On-Budget (2%)

Source: McKinsey Global Institute

Visualization: Horizontal Bar Chart
Cause of Major Budget Variation:
Poor Early-Stage Estimation

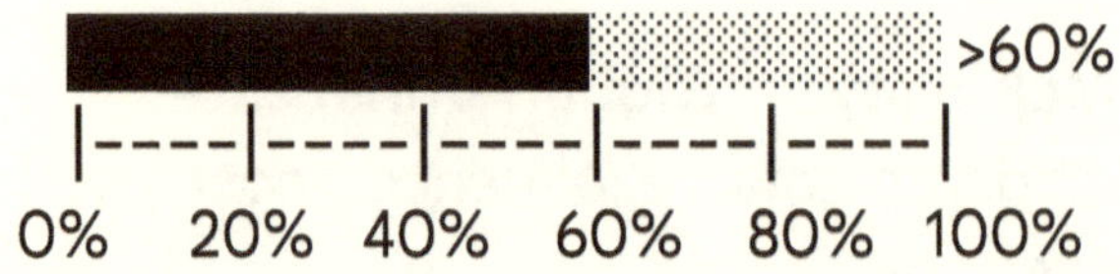

Source: PwC Global Construction Survey

1.2 Anatomy of Compounding Error

Every construction project moves through phases: concept, feasibility, design, tender, construction, and close-out. Each stage is built on the numbers established in the previous. When the initial assumptions are faulty—even by 1–2%—their impact multiplies. A 1% miscalculation made during conceptual design can multiply by three or more over the project lifecycle.

This fact is repeatedly confirmed by research from leading bodies like PMI, AACEI, and ENR. Estimates at the "fuzzy front end" of a project—typically AACEI Class 5 with a -50% to +100% accuracy range—set expectations, shape financing, and often determine which team wins the job. Inaccuracies at this stage ripple through procurement, scheduling, and delivery.

"Inaccurate estimates are not forgotten—they accumulate interest and come due when it hurts most." — *Project Controls Director, Dubai Giga-Project*

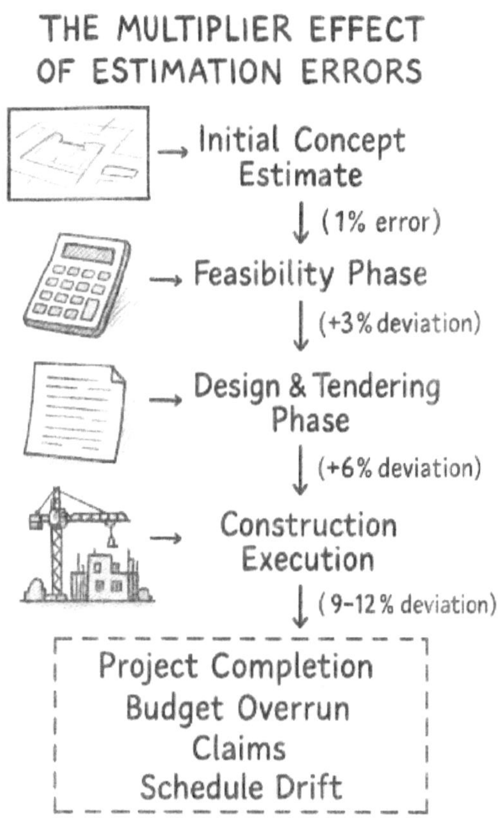

1.3 Real-World Lessons: Numbers Come Due

- **KSA Hospital Expansion, 2010–2016:** The initial estimate erred by just 1.7% due to underestimated soil remediation costs. This seemingly minor oversight, compounded by subsequent change orders and inflation, escalated to a budget breach of over 10% by project closeout.

- **Chicago Express Lanes, 2018:** A 2% underestimation of material transport distances spiralled into a near 100-day delay, triggering severe penalties and significant reputational fallout for the contractor.

1.4 The Organizational Feedback Loop

High-performing organizations treat estimation as a continuous, feedback-driven discipline. They continuously review and improve their estimation accuracy by institutionalizing lessons learned. This involves:

- **Estimate Autopsies:** Structured post-project sessions where cross-disciplinary teams review major deviations, analyze forecast versus actuals, and update norms.
- **Benchmarking Libraries:** Establishing and maintaining rigorous historical databases to recalibrate cost libraries, risk factors, and markups.
- **Incentives for Accuracy:** Rewarding teams for accurate forecasting and honest reporting, not simply for winning jobs with overly optimistic numbers.

WORLD-CLASS PRACTICE: PMI research shows that organizations investing in rigorous historical databases and regular estimate reviews can reduce their average cost deviation by up to 16% compared to industry peers.

1.5 Practical Strategies for Accuracy

To combat the multiplier effect and neutralize the cultural pressure to "sharpen the pencil," organizations should adopt the following strategies:

- **Establish an Estimate Autopsy Program:** Hold quarterly sessions led by cross-disciplinary teams to review major deviations and update internal benchmarks.
- **Leverage Reference Class Forecasting:** Anchor new estimates in the real historical performance of past projects, adjusting for unique risk factors, rather than relying on untested optimism.
- **Cultivate an Estimation Champion:** Appoint a senior expert responsible for enforcing standards and driving a culture of accuracy across the business.

1.6 Key Takeaways

- Even small early-stage errors act as force multipliers for cost and time overruns. Every 1% inaccuracy during early phases can multiply threefold or more by completion.

- Rigorous feedback loops, historical benchmarking, and a culture of honesty are essential to break the multiplier effect.
- Treat estimation not as a technical task, but as a strategic asset that forms the financial backbone of successful construction.

1.7 Real-Life Applications

1. Implement an "estimation maturity" assessment using AACEI's framework.
2. Initiate mandatory "Estimate Autopsies" after project closeout to capture and learn from every variance.
3. Replace flat-rate contingencies with quantified, scenario-based reserves built on historical risk data.

Chapter 2

From Ink-on-Linen to LIDAR—The Deep Evolution of Quantity Surveying

2.1 The Roots of Measurement: Building Trust in Early Construction

In 18th and 19th century Britain, the "measurer" was both detective and diplomat, safeguarding trust between landowners, architects, and craftsmen. These specialists painstakingly tallied every brick, timber, and cask of lime by candlelight—calculations inked on linen, tested by site walks, and disputed in smoke-filled coffee houses. As the Industrial Revolution unleashed an unprecedented construction boom, the limitations of this ad-hoc measurement became painfully clear.

> **Anecdote:** The building of London's St. Pancras station famously halted for days as two rival measurers haggled over the count of iron girders—the cost variation at stake was £20,000, a fortune at the time.

2.2 The Birth of Standardization: SMM, RICS, and a New Profession

The early 20th century witnessed a revolutionary

change. The United Kingdom pioneered the **Standard Method of Measurement (SMM)**, creating a uniform system for quantifying works that enabled competitive tendering and contract balance. This, combined with the professional status and ethical guidelines provided by the **Royal Institution of Chartered Surveyors (RICS)**, elevated the Quantity Surveyor (QS) from a trade role to a respected profession. RICS's **New Rules of Measurement (NRM)** series later ushered in a global era, blending traditional Bills of Quantities (BoQ) with life-cycle costing and sustainability targets.

2.3 The Internationalization of Quantity Surveying

By the mid-20th century, as mega-projects spread across the globe, so did these standards. This led to the development of other influential systems:

- **Saudi Aramco Engineering Standards (SAES):** Emphasize rigorous escalation logic, strict documentation, and deep sensitivity to project risk—now a gold standard for KSA giga-projects.
- **CSI MasterFormat:** Built for American construction, this divides work into 50 divisions and forms the backbone of cost comparison and bid evaluation for major US infrastructure.

Often, international teams must translate across these systems, creating hybrid matrices to keep global supply chains speaking a common financial language.

2.4 The Digital Revolution: From Spreadsheets to Drones

By the 1990s, spreadsheets replaced ledgers. But the real leap arrived with **Building Information Modeling (BIM)**. By linking three-dimensional models with time (4D) and cost (5D), QSs can now generate instant, scenario-adjusted BoQs. This is further enhanced by:

- **Laser Scanning/LIDAR:** Produces high-fidelity

as-built point clouds, critical for progress claims and retrofits.

- **Drones:** Provide fast, accurate mapping of site volumes and progress, improving measurement speed and claim substantiation.

  Case Example: A UK hospital redevelopment used LIDAR and drone scans to uncover legacy pipe runs missed in old plans, saving an estimated £800,000 and three months that would have otherwise been lost to rework.

2.5 The Modern QS Toolkit: Skills for the Next Era

Today's QS is no longer just a "counter of bricks"—they are contract architects, claims advisors, and commercial strategists. The modern toolkit demands a blend of:

- **Technical Skills:** High proficiency in BIM, LIDAR, and automated takeoff tools.
- **Commercial Acumen:** Deep contract and claims understanding, with the ability to structure innovative payment and risk-sharing systems.
- **Collaborative Abilities:** Mediation, cross-border team coordination, and stakeholder alignment.

- **Analytical Prowess:** Data curation, digital reporting, and the ability to translate measurement into actionable executive insights.

2.6 Key Takeaways

- Quantity Surveying evolved from on-site trust-building to an international standard-bearer, shaping the financial "language" of global construction.
- Today's QS blends deep domain knowledge, digital mastery, and strategic commercial influence.

- The future demands cross-standard fluency, technological adaptability, and a leadership mindset.

2.7 Real-Life Applications

1. Pilot drone-based progress measurement on your next project for live, claim-grade evidence.
2. Build a multi-standard translation table for your BoQs, leveraging cloud databases for collaborative, global inputs.
3. Launch a QS skills-upgrade program in your organization, integrating digital, commercial, and ESG cost curriculum.

Chapter 3

The Precision Estimation Pyramid—A Five-Level Framework

3.1 Why Estimation Demands a System, Not Just a Spreadsheet

Every time a project misses its mark, the postmortem reveals a common undercurrent: the estimate was only as strong as its weakest link. In high-stakes construction, estimation needs to be a transparent, defensible, and continuous process. The Precision Estimation Pyramid delivers this by turning estimation into a layered architecture, where each decision is built with confidence on the one below it.

> **"A great estimate isn't a single number; it's a system of truths—each layer informed by the last, and each decision owned."** — *Senior Cost Manager, European Infrastructure JV*

3.2 The Five Levels of the Pyramid

Level 1: Vision — Defining Project Success
Estimation begins not with a spreadsheet, but with dialogue. What is the client's true measure of victory? An opening date, a cost cap, a carbon benchmark? Without

clear targets, it is impossible to judge options or prioritize risk.

Level 2: Scope — From Fuzzy to Detailed

A robust Work Breakdown Structure (WBS), tied to information maturity (using AACEI's five-class estimate taxonomy), is the estimator's bulwark against "scope drift." Vague descriptions like "To be confirmed" are the silent killers of projects.

Level 3: Quantities — Digital and Physical Truths

Modern estimators harness BIM 5D, laser scans, and drone mapping to marry virtual intent with site reality. BoQs are continuously synchronized with design development and validated with reference projects or digital as-builts.

Level 4: Rates — Intelligent Costing

Rates come alive when tied to current market indices, vendor RFQ data, regional productivity curves, and even historical claims data that flags "risky" items. Never rely on a single opinion; benchmark rates against at least two reputable sources.

Level 5: Risk & Contingency — Dynamic, Data-Driven Buffering

The "flat 10% contingency" is a relic. Contemporary practice uses Monte Carlo simulations, layered contingencies (for design risk, market risk, etc.), and even AI-enhanced forecasting. Contingency should be visible, owned, and tracked as actively as any other cost code.

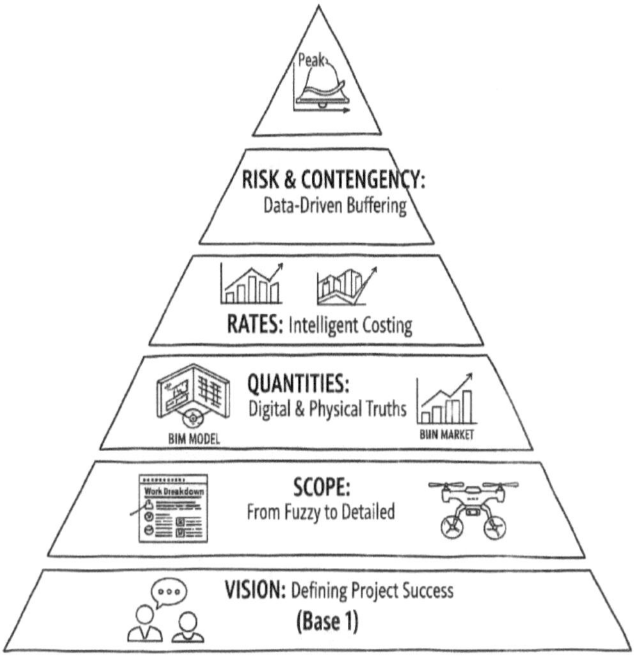

3.3 The Pyramid in Practice: A Mega-School in Mumbai

When the Mumbai Metropolitan Region tendered a 5,000-student school complex, a global JV applied the Pyramid. They:

1. Organized "success mapping" workshops with school officials (Vision).
2. Developed a Class 3 WBS mapped to local lessons-learned (Scope).
3. Engaged a 5D BIM specialist for real-time quantities (Quantities).

4. Benchmarked trade rates against five local and two international build-outs (Rates).
5. Applied scenario-based contingency using proprietary ML software (Risk).

Outcome: Their bid had a 3.5% contingency (vs. the state's default 10%) and delivered at less than 2% deviation from forecast—a rare feat in Indian social infrastructure.

3.4 Key Takeaways

- The Estimation Pyramid creates defensible, adaptable, and transparent forecasts that drive management confidence and client trust.
- Each layer addresses a classic source of project pain, from ambiguous goals to lazy contingency.
- This is not a theory: across KSA, the UK, and the US, this approach has proven to reduce average bid-to-delivery cost drift by 25–60%.

3.5 Real-Life Applications

1. Reverse-engineer your failed or overrun projects: where did the Pyramid break?
2. Mandate that every major bid submission includes a "Pyramid Compliance Checklist" documenting assumptions and data quality at each tier.
3. Use Pyramid logic to "audit" JV and consortium partner estimates to improve trust and joint accountability.

Chapter 4

International Rulebooks—PMI, AACEI, FIDIC, RICS, NEC3, CSI

4.1 Why Standards Matter: The Language of Global Construction

In construction, misunderstanding a rulebook can be costlier than misunderstanding a blueprint. As projects cross borders, the ability to "speak" PMI, AACEI, FIDIC, RICS, NEC, or CSI is not just a technical skill—it's the foundation of commercial trust, legal defensibility, and seamless project delivery. Without a common language, ambiguity fuels dispute.

4.2 The "Big Six" Frameworks at a Glance

Framework	Primary Focus	Best For
PMI PMBOK	Process & Knowledge Areas	Structuring project management and scope control.
AACEI TCM	Total Cost Management	Rigorous cost estimation, risk, and forensic analysis.
FIDIC	Contract	Defining risk

	Conditions	allocation and dispute resolution internationally.
RICS NRM	Measurement Rules	Standardizing BoQs and cost plans, especially in the UK/Commonwealth.
NEC3/4	Collaborative Contracts	Driving shared goals and proactive risk management.
CSI MasterFormat	Specification & Coding	Organizing work into divisions for US-based projects.

4.3 Bridging the Systems: The Reality of Multinational Delivery

Joint Ventures on giga-projects routinely need to translate between these systems. For example, a project might use:

- **FIDIC** for the main contract and claims.
- **RICS** for preparing the BoQs for payment.
- **CSI MasterFormat** for cost coding to align with a multinational supply chain's ERP system.

> **Practice Case: Riyadh Metro** The Riyadh Metro's North-South Line required a "translation matrix" developed by the project controls team. This matrix linked

every line item, cost code, risk register entry, and payment milestone across the FIDIC, RICS, and CSI frameworks being used by different partners.

4.4 Common Failure Modes

- **Mapping Errors:** Trades or scopes missed in translation between frameworks (e.g., RICS to CSI).
- **Dual Standards:** Applying different rules for risk or contingency, resulting in under- or over-allocation.
- **Cultural Clashes:** Local customs for claims or adjudication conflicting with international contract terms.

4.5 Success Factors for Cross-Border Work

- **Early Multi-Framework Workshops:** Bring all partners together to map differences and agree on a unified approach.
- **Appoint a "Framework Integrator":** A dedicated role on any JV whose sole job is translation, alignment, and governance.
- **Use a Common Data Environment (CDE):** Platforms like Aconex or Autodesk Construction Cloud allow for multi-standard tagging and a single source of truth.

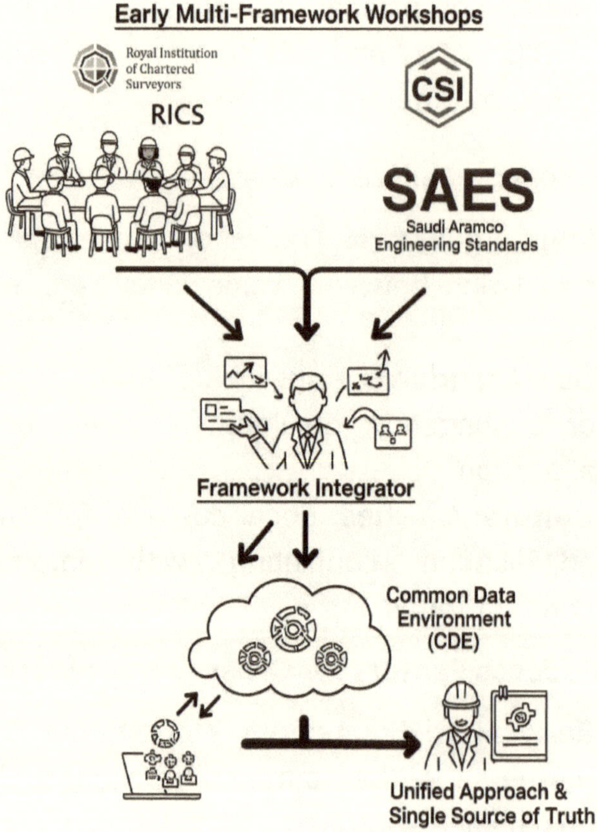

4.6 Key Takeaways

- International project success demands multi-framework fluency; alignment is a form of risk mitigation.
- Early mapping, unified data environments, and expert "translators" are mission-critical.
- As digital, ESG, and AI trends accelerate,

standards will become more interoperable, but the best teams will always know the strengths and quirks of each.

4.7 Real-Life Applications

1. Before every JV, build a translation matrix and conduct a system "war game"—test a bid scenario through each framework.
2. Run annual training refreshers for your team on new FIDIC amendments, NEC4 claim routes, or ICMS updates.

Chapter 5

Data-Driven Take-Offs—Digital Measurement and 5D BIM

5.1 The Take-Off Transformation: From Handhelds to Digital Clouds

Accurate quantity take-offs have always been the cornerstone of construction estimation. In the past, this was a laborious, manual task performed with scale rulers and highlighters, where human error was inevitable. Today, leading projects leverage Building Information Modeling (BIM), LIDAR scanning, and drone photogrammetry to produce continuously updating, dimensional, and verified quantity models.

5.2 Building Information Modeling (BIM) as a Game-Changer

BIM is more than just a 3D model. In best-in-class organizations, it is the live data source for estimation, progress claims, and procurement. The key is **5D BIM**:

- **3D:** Geometric spatial design.
- **4D:** Time and phasing (the schedule).
- **5D:** Cost and quantities, linked directly to the model.

Advantages:

- **Dynamic Quantities:** As designs evolve, so do

take-offs, closing the gap between "as planned" and "as built."

- **Clash Detection:** Automated tools flag conflicts between trades (e.g., HVAC vs. structural steel), catching millions in potential rework costs before they happen on site.
- **Traceability:** Every BoQ item can be traced back to its element in the design model, creating a clear audit trail for any changes.

> **Example:** On a London data center, integrating 5D BIM with the Common Data Environment (CDE) cut BoQ production time from three weeks to three days and enabled in-cycle scenario testing for different material options.

5.3 Drone and LIDAR-Enabled Surveys

Digital measurement truly shines in the field. High-precision drone flights and LIDAR scans can capture site conditions in hours, delivering:

- Up-to-date cut-and-fill volumes for fast-moving earthworks.
- Retrospective evidence for variations or claims.
- "Digital twins" that overlay planned progress against actual site conditions to spot slippage early.

5.4 Overcoming Adoption Barriers

While the benefits are clear, adoption faces challenges:

- **Training Gaps:** QS and field teams must learn new tools and workflows.
- **Data Interoperability:** Ensuring BIM, cost, and procurement systems "talk" to each other smoothly.
- **Upfront Investment:** The cost of hardware, software, and integration expertise.

The best approach is a hybrid rollout, where digital tools supplement, rather than replace, manual checks, allowing teams to build confidence and skills over time.

5.5 The Human Factor: The Augmented QS

Technology improves speed and accuracy, but it is the professional QS's insight—understanding constructability, validating model logic, and negotiating with vendors—that transforms raw data into value.

> **"Digital take-offs mean time saved, but the judgment to challenge a model or spot a missed detail is what turns a QS from a technician into a project strategist."** — *Cost Lead, KSA Giga-Project*

5.6 Key Takeaways

- 5D BIM, drones, and LIDAR have transformed take-offs from a manual slog into a dynamic, defensible, and value-adding process.
- The best teams blend technology with human insight, using digital tools to improve not just speed, but outcomes.
- The next frontier is full integration: linking take-offs, costs, schedules, claims, and carbon into a seamless project controls ecosystem.

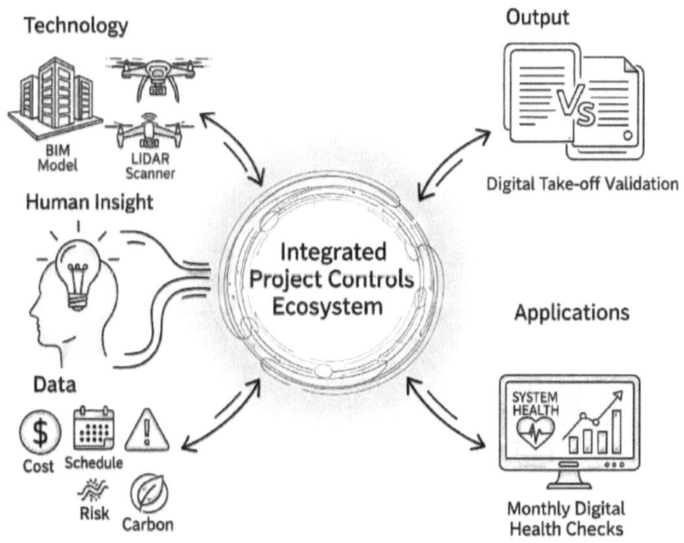

5.7 Real-Life Applications

1. On your next major bid, require a digital take-off

validation to be run side-by-side with the traditional method to compare accuracy and identify gaps.

2. Implement monthly "digital health checks" on your projects to ensure quantity models remain locked and traceable to the latest design and procurement data.

Part II:
Strategy and Execution

Chapter 6

Tendering Strategy and the 5-Layer Bid-Win Model

6.1 The Tendering Arena—Where Value is Won or Lost

In construction, the tender is far more than a pricing exercise; it is the moment when strategy, relationships, reputation, and numbers converge. A careless bid can secure a contract destined to lose money. A savvy approach—rooted in deep client understanding and risk intelligence—wins work on the right terms and cements future partnerships.

6.2 The 5-Layer Bid-Win Model: A Roadmap for Strategic Pursuits

Success in competitive tendering is rarely an accident. The world's most consistent winners follow a deliberate framework, which can be summarized as the 5-Layer Bid-Win Model.

Layer 1: Market Intelligence — Knowing the Battlefield Before the first spreadsheet is opened, top bidders perform exhaustive reconnaissance:

- **Client Needs:** What is the client's real pain point? Speed, innovation, transparency, or simply price?

- **Competition Scan:** Who will you face? What is their track record and bidding strategy?
- **Precedent Intelligence:** What happened on the last similar tenders? Were there disputes or notorious claims?

Layer 2: Price Architecture — Designing the Offer The best bids decompose price, showing not just a competitive total but a rationale for escalation, options, and risk-sharing. This includes a clear breakdown of base cost, provisional sums, alternates, and escalation factors, matched to the client's priorities.

> **Case Example:** For the Riyadh Metro, one consortium explicitly detailed its cost escalation formula based on ENR indices and separated out "design risk premiums." This transparency reassured the client and de-risked future disputes, helping them outscore two lower-priced bids on technical merit.

Layer 3: Technical Storytelling — More Than a Method Statement The technical submission is your opportunity to tell a story of certainty and innovation. Use 4D/5D BIM simulations, safety visualizations, and compelling case studies to demonstrate your capability and showcase your "value engineering" wins.

Layer 4: Governance Hygiene — Bulletproofing Compliance Rejections at the first legal or technical threshold are common and brutal. The best teams are obsessed with checklists, ensuring every submission is verified against the RFP's spirit and letter. They proactively address red flags like unbalanced BoQs or unrealistic schedules.

Layer 5: Relationship Capital — Beyond the Spreadsheet Trust and reputation still matter. Teams that invest in early and consistent engagement—through industry briefings, consultations, or collaborative pre-contract workshops—shape the client's perceptions long before pricing is reviewed.

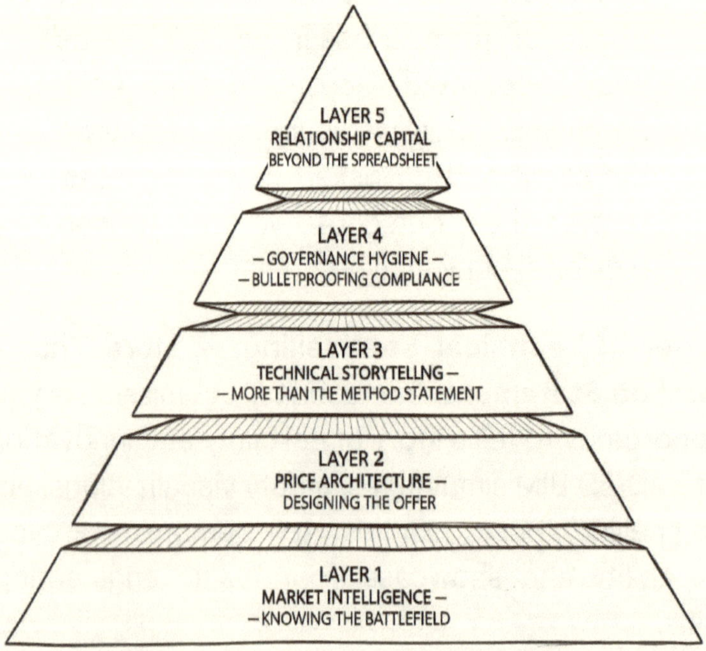

6.3 Common Traps and Red Flags

- **"Pricing to win":** Sacrificing risk or margin to get the award, only to bleed money on changes and claims later.
- **"Boilerplate" submissions:** Using flat, uninspiring technical write-ups copied from previous bids.
- **Siloed teams:** Commercial, technical, and legal teams working in isolation, missing the chance to craft a single, coherent story.

6.4 Key Takeaways

- Tendering is a strategic pursuit—layered, rehearsed, and client-centric.
- The 5-Layer Bid-Win Model transforms your approach from price-chasing to intelligent, value-led winning.
- Invest as much in relationships as in spreadsheets; trust and transparency often win tie-breaks.

6.5 Real-Life Applications

1. Before your next major bid, hold a dedicated Market Intelligence and Relationship Mapping session with your team.
2. Build a "Wine Cellar" library of your best, proven technical stories and case studies, and discard

any that didn't help close a sale or solve a dispute.

3. Run "war games" with your bid team, scenario-testing your submission against a hypothetical "killer" client evaluation.

Chapter 7

Red Flags & Black Swans—Tender Evaluation and Risk Signaling

7.1 The High Stakes of Risk Detection in Tendering

For both clients and bidders, tendering is a test of risk judgment. Those reviewing bids sift through submissions for signals: which offeror understands and has priced for risk, which is poised for claims, and which has left traps for themselves or the client. A single missed red flag can turn a profitable contract into a litigious nightmare.

7.2 Core Red Flags—What Experienced Evaluators See First

- **Unbalanced BoQs:** Items that are notably overpriced or underpriced. Overweighting early-phase activities (like site set-up) often presages cash flow games or future claims on underpriced change items.
- **Excessive Provisional Sums:** When more than ~15% of the contract value is in "provisional sums," it signals either design vagueness or a bidder's avoidance of scoping real risk.
- **Unrealistic Schedules:** Program durations that

are significantly tighter than market benchmarks signal either wishful thinking or an intent to win the award and rely on extensions of time later.

- **Unqualified Supply Chain:** Key subcontracts left unnamed or without clear vetting foreshadow delivery risk.
- **Unaddressed Market Risks:** Bids that fix prices for volatile commodities like steel or fuel without clear escalation or hedging clauses are time bombs.

> **Forensic Insight:** A global disputes survey by PwC found that 57% of major construction claims originated in unclear or unaddressed risks at the tender stage.

7.3 The Black Swan Problem—Beyond the Probable

A "black swan" is an event with low probability but extreme impact, such as the COVID-19 pandemic, which upended long-held assumptions about labor mobility and supply chains. What sets world-class teams apart is not that they can foresee every black swan, but that they openly scenario-plan, price for flexibility, and document "unknown unknowns" as part of their risk allowance.

> **"You win the best jobs not by pretending there's no risk, but by showing the client how you'll deal with**

> **the worst."** — *Risk Director, GCC International EPC JV*

7.4 The Advanced Risk Signaling Playbook

- **Peer Reviews:** Before every final bid, run dedicated "red flag" workshops with outside experts to stress-test the submission.
- **Quantitative Risk Registers:** Attach a quantified, line-by-line risk register (using tools like Primavera Risk Analysis or @Risk) as part of the technical offer to demonstrate transparency.
- **Early Engagement:** Use clarification meetings and Q&A sessions to surface unclear risks and secure written responses from the client.
- **Scenario Testing:** Present at least one scenario of significant disruption and demonstrate your team's agility and recovery plan.

THE ADVANCED RISK SIGNALING PLAYBOOK

7.5 Key Takeaways

- Red flags are silent signals to both the evaluator and the bid writer about where projects will win or lose in reality.
- Black swan resilience is a key differentiator; bid teams must scenario-plan, clarify, and document their risk agility.
- World-class tendering is as much about risk signaling and management as it is about technical prowess or price.

7.6 Real-Life Applications

1. Make risk peer reviews a non-negotiable milestone in your bid process before final submission.
2. Build a historical "risk archive" from your past projects to inform the risk matrices for future bids.
3. Offer clients voluntary risk workshops post-bid to build trust and show you are a transparent, long-term partner.

Chapter 8

Project Controls in Practice—Cost, Schedule, Risk, Procurement

8.1 The Essence of Modern Project Controls

Project controls are the heartbeat of multidisciplinary construction delivery. They are not just about data collection or compliance checklists—they are the nervous system of a successful project, integrating real-time analytics, intuitive dashboards, and proactive interventions across cost, schedule, risk, and procurement. At their best, controls transform a reactive process into proactive, data-driven strategy, creating the early warnings that preserve margin and reduce disputes. In the most advanced organizations, controls are not tacked onto project delivery; they shape decisions—from the boardroom to the site hut.

8.2 From Cost Reports to Control "Cockpits"

The days of relying on monthly cost reports that lagged weeks behind field reality are over. Today's best-in-class organizations use live dashboards and integrated "control cockpits" that aggregate data from financial systems, scheduling tools, procurement portals, and field apps.

These unified decision rooms synthesize status, trends, and live risks into a single source of truth. Trigger mechanisms are often built-in, linking dashboard thresholds directly to actions. For instance, if the Cost Performance Index (CPI) drops below a preset threshold like 0.95, a detailed variance review is automatically initiated.

While these principles of integrated controls are universal, their application varies in intensity. To see how the four pillars of controls are put into practice at the highest level, we will now take a deep dive into the rigorous model required on major EPC projects, particularly those adhering to client frameworks like Saudi Aramco's, where invoice rejections can delay project cash flow significantly.

8.3 A Deep Dive: The Aramco EPC Controls Model

Mastering project controls in a demanding EPC environment requires a deep understanding of how engineering, procurement, and construction interlink. It's about creating clarity and momentum through structure, visibility, and early anticipation. Let's break down the foundational concepts every EPC project controls professional is expected to master.

8.3.1 The Lifecycle of Engineering & Procurement

Engineering in an EPC project progresses through distinct phases:

1. **Concept Design:** High-level options and preliminary configurations are assessed.
2. **Pre-FEED:** The project's technical direction is validated, forming an early equipment list and layout concepts.
3. **FEED (Front-End Engineering Design):** The scope is firmly defined to a level sufficient for EPC tendering, producing key documents like PFDs and datasheets.
4. **Detailed Engineering:** All execution-level deliverables, such as IFC (Issued for Construction) drawings, are produced.
5. **As-Built:** Field-verified documents are issued to reflect the final constructed state.

Throughout this process, formal reviews at **30%, 60%, and 90% engineering completion** provide critical freeze points for alignment and issue resolution.

Critical Review Gates

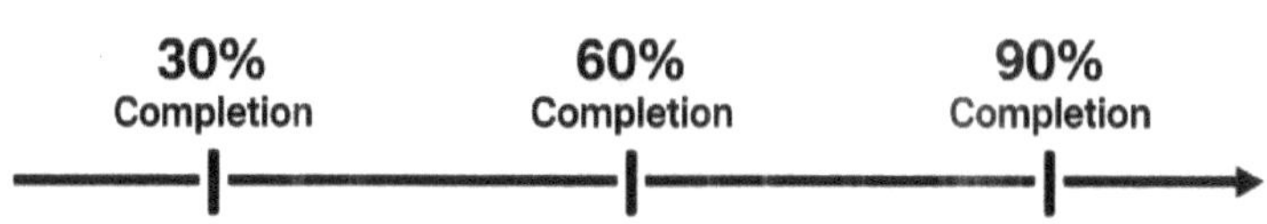

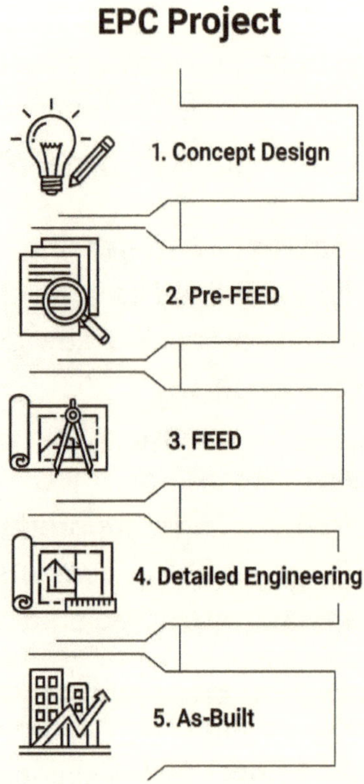

Parallel to this, the EPC procurement lifecycle unfolds in seven distinct stages:

1. **Requisitioning:** The engineering team prepares and gets approval for Material Requisitions (MRs) or Non-Material Requisitions (NMRs) for specialized items. This stage is critical as it formally defines what needs to be purchased.
2. **Purchasing & Award:** The procurement team issues Purchase Orders (POs), evaluates bids, and handles technical clarifications before

awarding a contract to a supplier.

3. **Vendor Documentation:** After the award, the vendor submits manufacturing drawings for approval, a crucial step to ensure items meet project specifications before fabrication begins.
4. **Manufacturing & Inspection:** The vendor begins manufacturing, during which inspections like the Factory Acceptance Test (FAT) are conducted to verify quality.
5. **Expediting & Logistics:** This stage involves managing the physical movement of goods from the factory to the project site. For long-lead items, this is often on the project's critical path.
6. **Site Receiving:** Materials are formally received at the site and tracked using Material Receiving Reports (MRRs).
7. **Inventory & Issuance:** Received materials are managed in a warehouse and issued to construction teams as needed, completing the cycle.

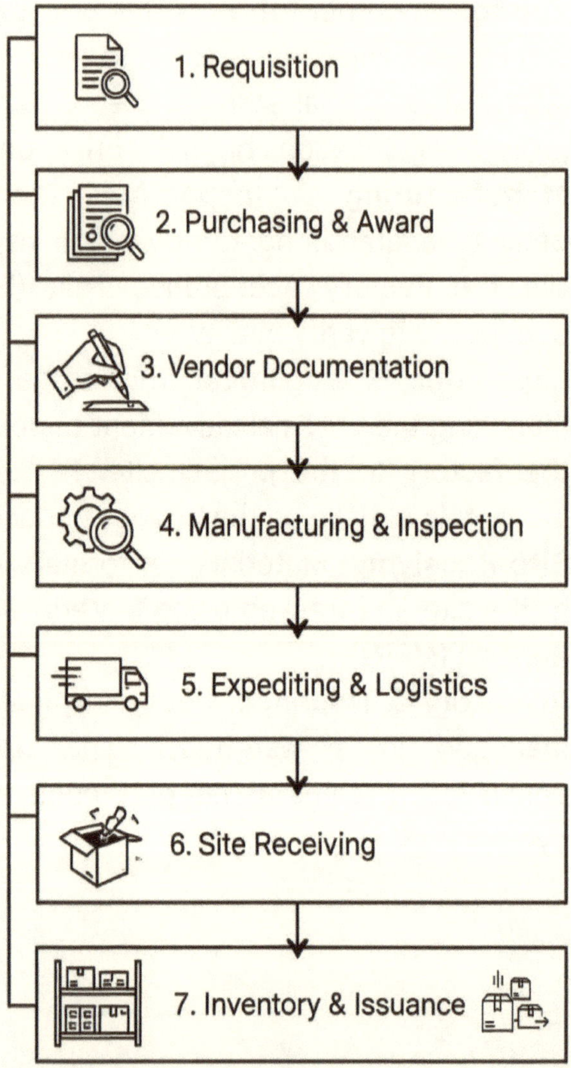

8.3.2 Engineering Deliverables and Progress Measurement

Each engineering discipline produces distinct deliverables, which are typically structured in

Primavera P6 under a discipline-wise Work Breakdown Structure (WBS).

- **Process:** PFDs, P&IDs, heat & material balances.
- **Mechanical:** Equipment specifications, layout drawings.
- **Piping:** Isometrics, MTOs, routing plans.
- **Electrical:** Single line diagrams (SLDs), load schedules, cable routing.
- **Instrumentation:** Loop diagrams, instrument indexes, IO lists.
- **Civil/Structural:** General arrangement (GA) drawings, foundation details, structural steel designs.

Progress for these deliverables is not measured by completion alone but by assigning weights to key stages. A typical structure allocates:

- **20% to IFD (Issued for Design)**
- **60% to IFC (Issued for Construction)**
- **20% to As-Built**

This allows for granular tracking. For example, if a project has 100 deliverables and 30 have been issued for construction, the earned progress is calculated as 30 items × 60% weight, equalling 18% of the total engineering progress for that set of deliverables.

8.3.3 Procurement Controls: Milestones, NMRs, and Long-Lead Items

Procurement progress is tracked using a milestone-based credit system, which is essential for linking progress to invoicing and cash flow. Progress is earned incrementally:

- **MR Approval:** A small credit is earned (usually 5%).
- **PO Issuance:** This milestone typically accounts for around 30% of the progress.
- **Vendor Drawing Approval & FAT:** Intermediate credit is given for these steps.
- **Delivery to Site:** This often carries the highest weight, around 40%. For a $1 million item, its delivery could represent $400,000 in earned value.

A critical component of EPC procurement is the **Non-Material Requisition (NMR)**. NMRs are used for specialized engineering materials that are not standard bulk items, such as instruments, skids, or special pipeline components. Despite being "non-material," they are critical to commissioning and are tracked with the same rigor as major equipment. Client standards, like those from Saudi Aramco, often require that all engineering materials with NMRs be tied to specific schedule activities to ensure full transparency and integration. This contrasts with non-engineering materials (like tools or PPE) and bulk materials (like concrete or rebar), which are procured via direct POs or tracked through consumption reports.

Key Concept: Common NMRs in Oil & Gas Pipeline Projects

- **Pig Signallers:** Detects the passage of a pipeline inspection gauge ("pig").
- **Corrosion Monitoring Systems:** Measures the rate of pipe corrosion.
- **Barred Tees:** A special fitting that allows pig passage through a future connection point.
- **Monolithic Isolation Joints (MIJs):** Electrically isolates sections of a pipeline for corrosion control.
- **Actuators:** The motor used to automate a valve.
- **Cathodic Protection Transformer Rectifiers:** The power supply for the corrosion prevention system.
- **Remote Terminal Units (RTUs):** The field computer that sends pipeline data back to the central control room.
- **Custody Transfer Metering Skids:** A certified, high-accuracy metering system used for billing clients.

8.3.4 Schedule Controls and the Critical Path

The **Critical Path** is the sequence of activities that determines the project's total duration. Any delay to an activity on this path will directly delay the entire project, as these activities have zero float (or slack). The critical path is dynamic and can shift during execution. It might begin with long-lead engineering deliverables (e.g., datasheets for a major compressor), move through the procurement cycle for that compressor, and finally end with its installation and commissioning activities. Managing the critical path requires constant monitoring and re-evaluation to proactively address constraints and slippages.

8.3.5 Tying It All to Invoicing: The Rules of Credit (RoC)

On major projects, progress is not just an internal metric; it directly drives billing. The **Rules of Credit (RoC)** are the contractually agreed-upon terms that define how progress translates into payment.

- **For Engineering:** Clients typically approve staged progress payments based on milestones like 20% for IFD, 60% for IFC, and 20% for As-Built.
- **For Procurement:** The RoC might award 30% upon PO issuance and 40% upon site delivery, with the remaining 30% spread across intermediate milestones like vendor document approval or FAT.

Aligning the schedule's progress measurement

system with the contractual Rules of Credit is absolutely essential for accurate cash flow forecasting and timely invoicing. A mismatch can lead to invoice rejections and severe cash flow problems for the contractor.

Case Study: A Level IV Schedule for a Saudi Aramco Pipeline Project

To illustrate how these concepts come together, the following is a representative extract from a Level IV Work Breakdown Structure (WBS) for a pipeline project. A Level IV schedule breaks down the project into detailed work packages and specific activities, forming the basis for weekly and monthly progress reporting, resource allocation, and invoicing. This level of detail is standard for managing complex EPC projects under frameworks like Aramco's.

1.0 Project Management

- **1.1 Project Controls & Reporting**
    - 1.1.1 Schedule Management
        - 1.1.1.2 Develop & Issue Level IV Schedule
        - 1.1.1.3 Weekly Schedule Updates & Lookaheads

    - 1.1.2 Cost Management & Invoicing
        - 1.1.2.1 Submit Monthly Progress Invoice to Aramco

2.0 Engineering

- **2.2 Process Engineering**
    - 2.2.1 P&ID Development
        - 2.2.1.2 Issue P&IDs for Aramco Review
        - 2.2.1.3 Issue P&IDs Issued for Construction (IFC)
- **2.4 Mechanical Engineering**
    - 2.4.1 Pig Launcher/Receiver Engineering
        - 2.4.1.1 Prepare Mechanical Datasheet
        - 2.4.1.2 Technical Bid Evaluation (TBE) of Vendor Offers
        - 2.4.1.3 Vendor Drawing Review & Approval
- **2.7 Instrumentation Engineering**
    - 2.7.1 Field Instrument Engineering
        - 2.7.1.2 Prepare Instrument Datasheets for all NMRs

3.0 Procurement

- **3.2 Long-Lead Items (LLI) - Mainline Valves**

- 3.2.1 Procurement Cycle - Mainline Valves
  - 3.2.1.2 Award Purchase Order (PO)
  - 3.2.1.4 Deliver Mainline Valves to Site
- **3.3 Bulk Materials - Line Pipe**
  - 3.3.1 Procurement Cycle - Line Pipe
    - 3.3.1.3 Deliver Line Pipe to Site - Lot 1

4.0 Construction

- **4.2 Right of Way (ROW)**
  - 4.2.1 ROW Preparation
    - 4.2.1.2 Clear & Grade ROW
- **4.3 Pipeline Installation**
  - 4.3.2 Mainline Welding
    - 4.3.2.1 Mainline Welding - Root & Hot Pass
  - 4.3.3 NDT & Repair
    - 4.3.3.1 Perform NDT (AUT/Radiography)
- **4.5 Tie-Ins**
  - 4.5.1 Mainline Section Tie-In Welds (Golden Welds)
    - 4.5.1.4 Execute "Golden Weld"

5.0 Pre-commissioning & Commissioning

- **5.1 Pre-commissioning Activities**
    - 5.1.1 Pipeline Section 1 Hydrotest
        - 5.1.1.2 Pressurize for Hydrotest - Section 1
- **5.2 Commissioning & Startup**
    - 5.2.1 System Handover
        - 5.2.1.2 Obtain Mechanical Completion Certificate (MCC)
    - 5.2.2 Startup Activities
        - 5.2.2.2 Introduce Hydrocarbons (First Gas/Oil)

6.0 Project Closeout

- **6.1 Final Documentation**
    - 6.1.1 Handover Dossier
        - 6.1.1.1 Compile As-Built Drawings
        - 6.1.1.3 Submit Final Dossier to Aramco

Key Project Milestones

Derived from the detailed schedule, these major milestones are what executive leadership and clients track to gauge overall project health. They often trigger major payments and signify the transfer of risk.

- **Engineering Milestones:**
    - 90% Engineering Model Review

    Complete
    - All "Issued for Construction" (IFC) Drawings Issued
- **Procurement Milestones:**
    - All Long-Lead Item (LLI) Purchase Orders (POs) Awarded
    - All Long-Lead Items (e.g., Valves, Pig Traps) Delivered to Site
- **Construction Milestones:**
    - 100% Right of Way (ROW) Cleared and Graded
    - 100% Mainline Welding and NDT Complete
    - Ready for Hydrotest
- **Commissioning & Handover Milestones:**
    - **Mechanical Completion Certificate (MCC):** The formal point where the client agrees the facility is built to spec and ready for commissioning.
    - **Ready for Introduction of Hydrocarbons:** The final step before the pipeline goes live.
    - **Provisional Acceptance Certificate (PAC):** Issued after successful startup, this signifies the beginning of the warranty period.

- **Final Acceptance Certificate (FAC):** The final milestone confirming all contractual obligations have been met.

8.4 The Human Engine—Culture, Skills, and Process

Technology does not replace discipline—it augments it. The best control teams:

- **Foster a transparent, blameless culture:** Issues are flagged early, not hidden until it's "too late."
- **Cross-train their staff:** Schedulers understand cost implications, and cost analysts appreciate risk management.
- **Embed controls from day one:** Controls are viewed not as a policing function, but as essential team decision-support.

> "Weekly dashboards don't just track—they trigger action, drive accountability, and make risk everyone's job, not just someone else's." — *Controls Director, GCC Giga-Project*

8.5 Key Takeaways

- Unified project controls, integrating cost, schedule, risk, and procurement, are essential for early deviation detection, margin protection, and informed decision-making.

- Live dashboards and proactive monitoring are standard practice in high-performing organizations; silos are fatal.
- Culture underpins success. Controls only work if teams trust the data, act on the insights, and own the numbers collectively.

8.6 Real-Life Applications

1. Set up a control cockpit using a tool like Power BI for your next project, linking cost, schedule, and risk KPIs.
2. Hold weekly "control huddles"—short, focused meetings driven by data and focused on early warning signals.
3. Use control KPIs as the basis for incentive and disincentive structures with both site and support staff.

Chapter 9

Toolbelt Mastery—Primavera P6, MS Project, Power BI Dashboards

9.1 The Digital Toolkit for Mastery, Not Just Compliance

Project controls are only as good as the tools that knit data and people together. In the digital era, mastery of your toolbelt is a defining feature of the world's top construction teams. But tools alone do not guarantee success; integration, user fluency, and the discipline to challenge the numbers are what extract real value.

9.2 Primavera P6—The Nerve Center of Complex Scheduling

Primavera P6 is the gold standard for the world's largest and most complex construction schedules. It empowers planning teams to:

- Build multi-thousand activity schedules for giga-projects.
- Define the Critical Path and manage float.
- Resource and cost-load activities for true Earned Value Management (EVM).
- Run "what-if" analysis to model delays and recovery strategies.

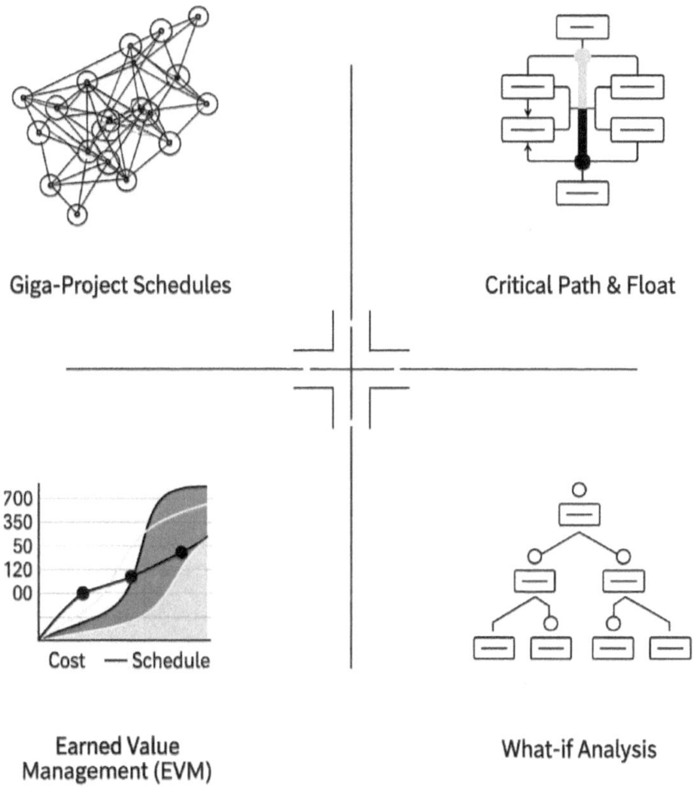

9.3 Microsoft Project—Agility for Mid-sized Projects

MS Project remains the trusted platform for mid-scale programs, valued for its rapid setup and familiar interface. Its strengths lie in:

- **Quick Mobilization:** Intuitive for non-planners, enabling design and site teams to own their parts of the schedule.
- **Rolling Wave Planning:** Perfect for phased

delivery or fast-track fit-out projects.

- **Cloud Integration:** Office 365 integration allows for real-time collaboration and communication.

9.4 Power BI—Visibility, Insight, and Action

Power BI has revolutionized project reporting, transforming static monthly PDFs into living, interactive dashboards. It enables:

- **Live KPI Dashboards:** Real-time updates of cost, schedule, procurement, and risk.
- **Customized Views:** Executive and site-level views ensure everyone sees the right data.
- **Drill-down Capability:** Go from a summary S-curve to an individual cost code in a few clicks.
- **Automated Alerts:** Triggers when KPIs breach preset thresholds (e.g., CPI falls below 0.95).

Live KPI Dashboards

Customized Views

Drill-down Capability

Automated Alerts

9.5 Integrating the Toolbelt—No Data "Islands"

The real power is not in using each tool in isolation, but in their synergy. Data must flow seamlessly between them. For example, critical path and earned value data from Primavera P6 should be exported nightly to update C-suite dashboards in Power BI.

9.6 Change Management: Enabling Adoption

Digital adoption stalls when tools are imposed without support. To succeed:

- **Onboard Early & Train Continuously:** Launch every project with hands-on tool workshops.
- **Celebrate Data Wins:** Publicly share stories where a live dashboard insight averted a risk or saved money.
- **Encourage Debate:** Make challenging or correcting a dashboard datum a badge of honor, not insubordination.

9.7 Key Takeaways

- Mastery of Primavera P6, MS Project, and Power BI is foundational, but integration and user discipline are what amplify results.
- Continuous training and a culture of data-driven action convert tech investment into a performance advantage.
- The next generation of tools will be smarter and more predictive but will always depend on user

judgment.

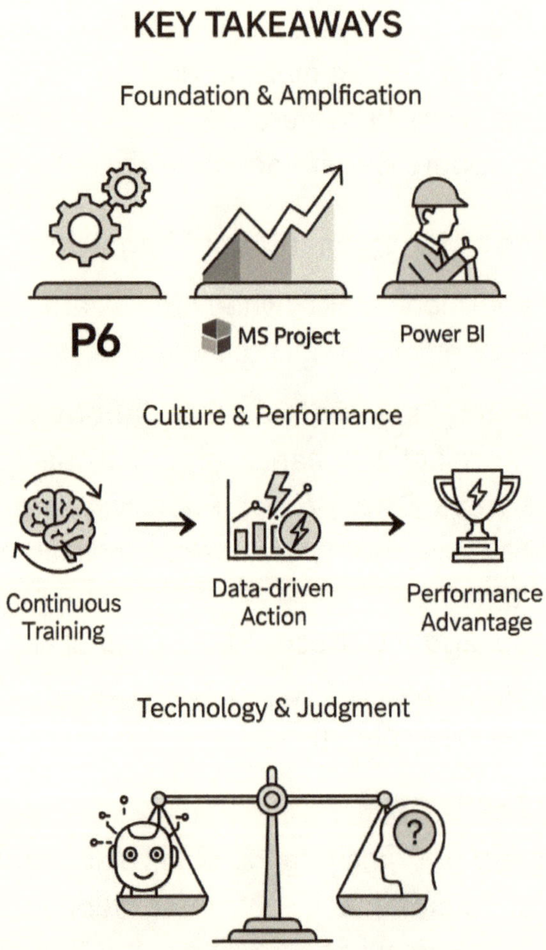

9.8 Real-Life Applications

1. Make Power BI the heartbeat of your next control room, linking every tool possible for live, actionable insight.

2. Demand that every planner and controls professional complete regular refresher training and tool certifications.
3. Hold weekly “dashboard dialogues”—an open session for any team member to challenge or update key numbers.

Part III:

Navigating Modern Realities

Chapter 10

Inflation, Volatility, and Post-COVID Supply Shocks

10.1 The Storm That Won't Pass: Construction's New Volatility

The 2020s have rewritten the rules of construction risk. Inflation surged globally, with costs for steel, copper, lumber, and labor spiking in unpredictable cycles. COVID-19, war, and sanctions exposed deep fragility in procurement strategies. As the World Economic Forum notes, material price shocks and logistics bottlenecks have swung tender price indices by double digits annually in some regions.

> **"Yesterday's cost plan became tomorrow's headline risk. If you aren't pricing volatility, you're gambling, not estimating."** — *Senior Estimator, GCC Giga-Project*

10.2 Key Risks and Transmission Mechanisms

- **Material Cost Spikes:** Global steel and timber prices doubled in 2021-22.
- **Labor Shortages:** Vaccine mandates, travel restrictions, and wage escalations depleted skilled labor pools across the GCC, UK, US,

Southeast Asia, and other key construction hubs worldwide.

- **Currency Fluctuations:** Multi-currency contracts saw wild swings in foreign exchange exposure.
- **Geopolitical Shocks:** War and export controls changed risk premiums overnight.

10.3 Mitigating the Unpredictable—Tools and Tactics

- **Flexible Escalation Clauses:** Shift from hard lump-sum deals to indexed, formula-based contracts referencing ENR or regional indices.
- **Early Supplier Commitment:** Secure long-lead equipment and critical materials at bid award, even before the design is fully finalized.
- **Alternative Sourcing & Modularity:** Develop "dual vendor" strategies or shift to modular/off-site solutions that can bypass congested shipping lanes.
- **Scenario-Based Risk Modeling:** Use Monte Carlo simulations to model multiple market conditions and update contingency models weekly.
- **Agility in Design:** Mandate "design for substitution" so that supply chain gaps can be bridged with alternate materials without triggering design chaos.

MITIGATING THE UNPREDICTABLE--TOOLS AND TACTICS

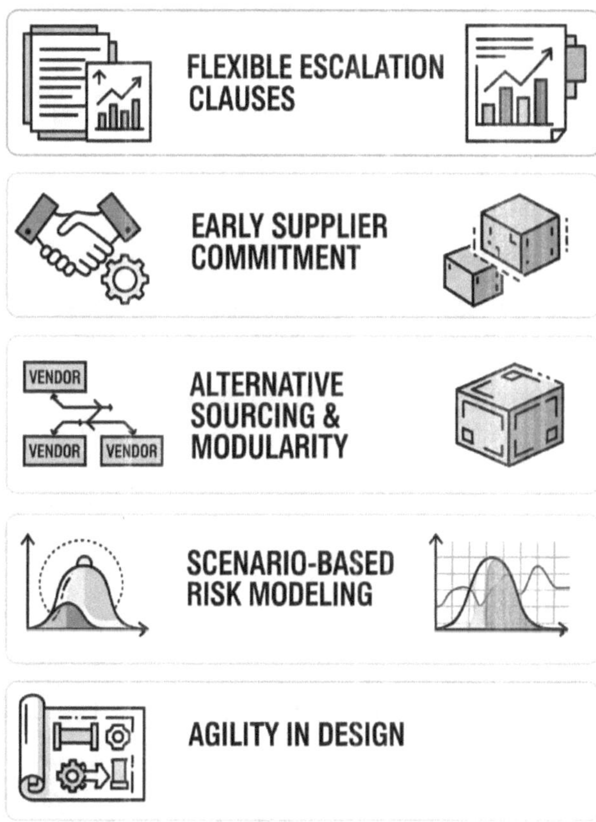

Case Story: Dubai Logistics Hub, 2021 The project faced an 85% surge in rebar prices mid-construction. The JV had pre-negotiated an index-linked escalation clause with the client and suppliers, sharing the risk above a 10% fluctuation. This contract flexibility allowed for rapid renegotiation, clawing back 60% of the unplanned cost.

10.4 Key Takeaways

- Volatility is now a baseline assumption, not an exception.
- Resilient organizations embrace indexed contracts, rapid risk modeling, and flexible procurement.
- Early and transparent dialogue with clients on risk-sharing is crucial for survival, not just profit.

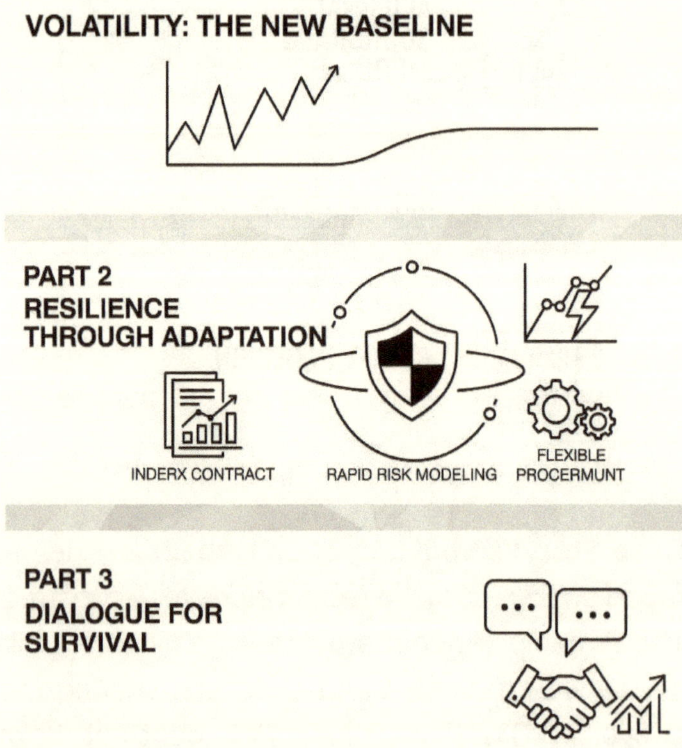

10.5 Real-Life Applications

1. Initiate a "volatility council" in your project office to meet weekly and review market exposure.
2. Pilot a dual-sourcing strategy for your highest-risk long-lead package on the next bid.
3. Roll new escalation and force majeure templates into your standard contract library for all new pursuits.

Chapter 11

Stakeholder Conflicts, Scope Creep, and the Politics of Change

11.1 Construction Is Conflict: The Project as an Arena

Every large project is a collision of interests. Owners want maximum value for minimum cost. Designers chase innovation. Contractors optimize for time and margin. Regulators enforce compliance. Add financiers, end-users, and local communities, and you get a web where misalignment is not an "if" but a "when."

> **"Scope is not a number; it's a battlefield. Each change echoes across budget, schedule, and trust."** — *PMO Head, KSA Giga-Project*

11.2 The Anatomy of Scope Creep

Scope creep—the silent killer of budgets—typically emerges in three ways:

1. **Client-Driven Changes:** New end-user needs or regulatory requirements introduced after the contract is finalized.

2. **Designer-Driven Evolution:** Specification drift as new technologies or aesthetic ideas emerge mid-design.
3. **Execution-Led Variations:** Site realities (like unforeseen ground conditions) that clash with design assumptions.

> **Case: UK Hospital Build** A £1 billion hospital endured over 850 formal change events. Despite a tight baseline, the final cost drifted 19% higher, with 96% of the overrun attributed to scope creep and change management failures.

11.3 The Politics of Change: Power and Process

Informal influence from senior sponsors or political officials can often bypass formal change control processes. To counter this, leading projects on giga-developments like Dubai Expo and NEOM have instituted **Change Control Boards**—cross-functional stakeholder bodies with the authority to review, cost, and approve all changes. Projects with strong boards see lower levels of claims and faster delivery.

11.4 Rigorous Change Control: Process and Mindset

The essentials of effective change control include:

- **A Clear Change Protocol in the Contract:**

Defines rules for notification, costing, and client sign-off.

- **Baseline Lock and Documentation:** All parties sign off on the initial scope, and version control is religiously maintained.
- **Digital Tools:** Integrated platforms like Aconex or Oracle Unifier ensure all change events are logged, tracked, and impact-analyzed.
- **Root Cause Analysis:** Every major change should generate a learning review to improve future processes.

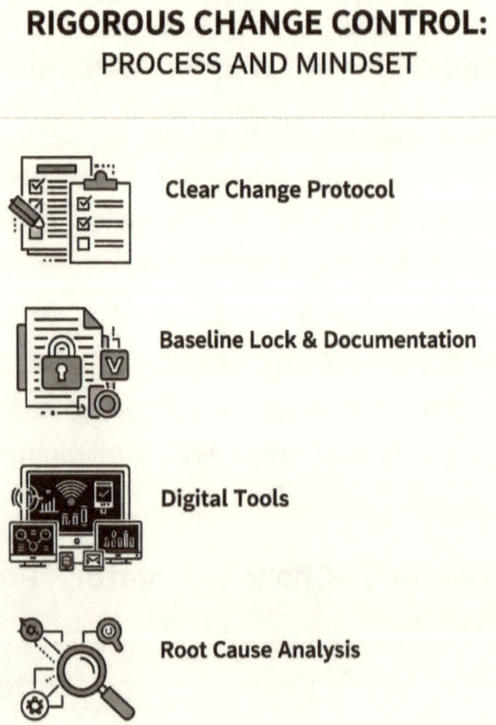

11.5 Key Takeaways

- Every project is a negotiation; stakeholder mapping and process discipline are essential to manage the politics of change.
- Scope management is a team sport—adversarial practices are expensive, while collaborative models outperform.
- Change isn't just noise—it's a pulse of project health. Track it, analyze it, and learn from it.

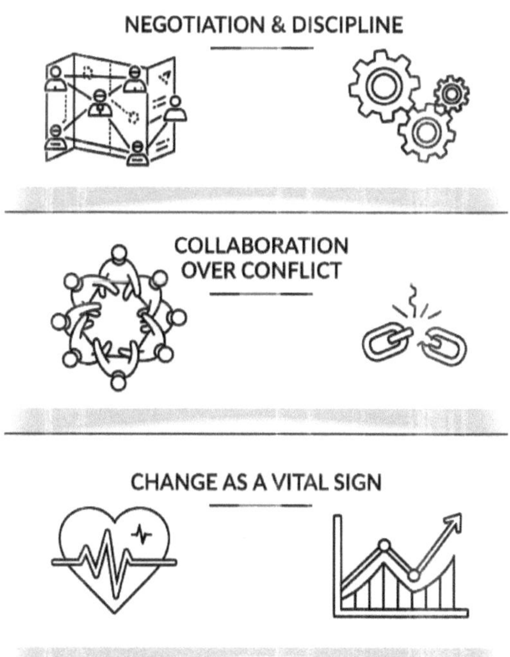

11.6 Real-Life Applications

1. Make stakeholder mapping and change risk workshops mandatory at every project phase gate.
2. Integrate your change logs with live impact dashboards and review them weekly with the project leadership team.
3. Run post-project "conflict and change" lessons-learned sessions and update your controls and contract playbooks continuously.

Chapter 12

AI, Automation & Ethics—From Machine-Learned Contingencies to Carbon Twins

12.1 The Tipping Point: Why AI Is Changing Project Controls Forever

Artificial Intelligence (AI), automation, and predictive analytics are no longer peripheral innovations—they are becoming operational essentials in construction. What triggered this shift?

- **Data explosion:** Every project now generates terabytes of structured and unstructured data—from schedules, site photos, and RFIs to procurement logs and change orders.
- **BIM maturity:** Widespread 4D/5D BIM adoption means there is now a synchronized digital model of cost and time.
- **Market pressure:** Clients demand faster delivery, transparent costing, and carbon accountability. AI is emerging as the only way to meet all three simultaneously.

In 2023, Skanska UK integrated an AI-driven forecasting engine with their cost database and project dashboards. The result? A 21% improvement in early identification of scope-level risk deviations—weeks before conventional indicators would have flagged them.

We're entering an era where **earned value is validated by drones, carbon is calculated in real-time, and contingencies are released by scenario simulators—not guesswork.**

12.2 Practical Applications: AI and Automation Across the Project Lifecycle

1. Machine Learning for Cost and Risk Forecasting

AI is helping teams move from reactive variance tracking to proactive deviation prediction.

Example: On a gas processing project in Jubail, a contractor applied AI to past project data to model material cost volatility and subcontractor performance. The model flagged a high-risk package where the subcontractor had a history of late mobilization. Mitigation actions taken two months ahead prevented schedule drift—something traditional lookaheads had missed.

Key Benefits:

- Detect "silent" patterns of risk: e.g., unresponsive vendors, RFI clusters, repeated QS variations.
- Create dynamic risk models that evolve with

project data (weather, logistics, pricing).

2. Automated Measurement and Claims with Drone-AI Integration

Progress reporting is often disputed due to subjective assessments and delayed site updates. Now, drones with AI vision analytics are changing the game.

Example: In the Dubai South Logistics Park, a contractor used drone-based AI to map excavation volumes and structural progress daily. This reduced interim payment approval time from 14 days to 4—and eliminated 90% of claim disputes during early works.

What AI Adds:

- Objective, timestamped verification of work done (volumes, floor casting, façade progress).
- Integration with 5D BIM models for real-time earned value tracking.

3. Digital Twins and Carbon Twins for ESG Integration

Digital twins go beyond visual simulation—they now integrate carbon and cost forecasting.

Example: At the NEOM Oxagon site, design teams used a carbon twin to model 6 material options for a data center façade. By simulating both cost and CO_2

impact, they selected a hybrid steel-glass solution that cut emissions by 18% with only a 3% cost increase—validated in the BIM-linked procurement model.

Carbon Twins Enable:

- Scenario testing of low-carbon options before final design freeze.
- Embodied and operational carbon tracking as part of live project controls.

12.3 Realities and Limits: Human Judgment and Algorithmic Blind Spots

AI can be powerful—but it's not immune to failure. Field leaders must be aware of three common failure modes:

Model Dependence Without Understanding

On a Qatar metro extension, an AI model suggested cutting rebar quantities by 5% based on historical optimization. The QS team, sensing a mismatch with local seismic code, halted implementation. A manual re-check confirmed that local compliance rules weren't factored in.

AI can speed up bad decisions too—unless professionals stay engaged and vigilant.

Data Bias and Historical Flaws

In projects where contingency was habitually under-allocated to "look competitive," AI models trained on that data may perpetuate a risky optimism bias.

Mitigation: Teams must audit training datasets—weed out flawed assumptions, underreported claims, or politically adjusted S-curves.

Lack of Explainability in High-Stakes Environments

Especially in public sector or regulated infrastructure (airports, energy), AI decisions must be explainable. If a model allocates less contingency or flags early contract closure, teams must be able to justify "why" in boardrooms or audits.

12.4 Building the Ethical and Operational AI Framework

AI in construction controls should be guided by these four practical pillars:

1. Human-in-the-Loop Governance

No AI-driven recommendation should trigger commercial actions (like change orders or vendor disqualifications) without sign-off from domain experts.

Field Example: On a petrochemical expansion project in Ras Al-Khair, AI suggested early close-out of a vendor package. The controls manager flagged an unresolved NCR in the manual log—preventing a premature financial closure.

2. Digital Ethics Board

Multinational JVs (e.g., Korean–Gulf–European) often create internal review bodies to vet the use of predictive analytics in procurement, safety, and performance scoring.

- Ensure fairness, especially where AI ranks subcontractor capability.
- Flag cultural/legal red lines in data usage (e.g., facial recognition on-site may violate laws in some jurisdictions).

3. Data Security and Sovereignty

Construction data—particularly in defense, energy, or SEZ projects—is often sensitive. AI models must adhere to:

- Local data hosting laws (e.g., in Saudi Arabia under SDAIA guidelines)
- Encryption protocols for all personally identifiable data and financials
- Role-based access in shared environments (BIM 360, Aconex)

4. Auditability and Explainability by Default

Every algorithm that influences cost or risk decisions must:

- Log the input dataset, model version, and user interaction
- Produce a readable rationale for every high-impact output

12.5 Key Takeaways

1. AI is already reshaping the DNA of estimation and control—but only the teams that embrace both technology and accountability will reap sustainable benefits.
2. Risk, contingency, and progress validation are being redefined—from human intuition to data-backed decision engines.
3. Ethical integration is the differentiator—tools may be available to all, but trust, transparency, and explainability will define who leads the industry.

12.6 Real-Life Applications

- **Pilot AI Forecasting on Closed Projects**
  Select 2–3 recently closed projects and apply an AI cost/risk model. Compare its forecast accuracy with the original estimate to build internal confidence and identify model gaps.
- **Launch a "Carbon Twin" Use Case**

On your next high-profile project, simulate at least 2 material or logistics choices using a digital twin that reports both cost and embodied carbon side-by-side.

- **Create a Digital Governance Charter**
  Before AI adoption scales, create a practical one-pager for your team: when AI can be trusted, when human review is mandatory, and how data is logged and secured.

Chapter 13

Modular, Off-Site, and the Rise of Productized Construction

13.1 Why Modularity Now? A Revolution Decades in the Making

For over a century, construction was defined by its site-based, labor-intensive nature. But technology, supply chain globalization, and chronic productivity challenges have forced a rethink. Modular and off-site construction, once a niche, now drive the delivery of giga-projects, schools, hospitals, and high-tech data centers.

> **"Modularity isn't just about boxes delivered on trucks. It's the industrialization of building—predictability, speed, safety, and quality at a level site-by-site work can't match."** — *Modular Delivery Lead, UK Healthcare JV*

13.2 The Business Case: The Data and the Impact

- **Schedule Savings:** McKinsey data shows modular can reduce build time by 20–50%.
- **Cost Predictability:** Factory-built precision minimizes waste and rework, enabling fixed-price

guarantees.

- **Quality and Safety:** Controlled environments deliver higher QA and can cut accident rates by 50% or more.
- **ESG and Carbon:** Off-site processes generate less waste and typically have lower embodied carbon footprints.

Metric	Traditional Construction	Modular Construction
Schedule	Sequential, weather-dependent	Parallel, concurrent manufacturing
Waste	10-15% of materials	2-4% of materials
Safety	High-risk site environment	Controlled factory conditions
Quality	Variable, site-dependent	Standardized, high-precision

13.3 Real-World Case Studies

- **Birmingham Modular Tower:** Over 70% of the structure was assembled off-site, slashing the on-site program by seven months and reducing truck movements by 56%.
- **Riyadh Education Cluster:** Modular classrooms produced in Jeddah factories were installed

within weeks, syncing delivery with school term starts and freeing up labor for other infrastructure works.

13.4 The Digital Backbone: BIM and DfMA

The key enabler for modular construction is **Design for Manufacture and Assembly (DfMA)**. This approach requires early integration of designers, engineers, and manufacturers to ensure all components can be produced, shipped, and assembled efficiently. Modularity isn't bolted on; it's designed in from the start, using digital libraries of repeatable BIM objects.

13.5 Commercial and Risk Implications

Modular construction shifts the risk profile. It requires a longer, more intensive design phase and early vendor commitment. While it reduces weather and on-site safety risks, it increases sensitivity to logistics, port shutdowns, and module QA issues, requiring new contract models.

13.6 Key Takeaways

- Modular and off-site methods are a mainstream driver of time, cost, risk, and ESG advantages.
- Upfront integration, rigorous digital management, and a collaborative DfMA culture are essential for success.
- Productized construction is about more than

building—it's about industrializing project value.

13.7 Real-Life Applications

1. Assess every new bid or feasibility study for modular/OSM opportunities as a baseline, not an exception.
2. Co-locate your design and production teams in the early design phase to avoid "throwing it over the wall."
3. Build strategic partnerships with local fabricators or global OSM leaders to drive both pricing and design innovation advantages.

Chapter 14

Building with Carbon in Mind—ICMS 3 and ESG Costing

14.1 Green Is Now Gold: The Financial Imperative for Low-Carbon Construction

Net-zero commitments, shareholder activism, and evolving regulations have all converged to make carbon as critical a number as time, cost, or safety. ESG (Environmental, Social, and Governance) mandates now shape the terms of public tenders, private investments, and even insurance eligibility. Integrating carbon as a first-class project control variable is no longer just a compliance play—it's a major source of competitive advantage.

> **"Tomorrow's lowest bidder will often be today's lowest-carbon builder. It's not a trend, it's a requirement."** — *Sustainable Construction Director, Tier 1 Contractor, EU*

14.2 Introducing ICMS 3—The Universal Carbon-Cost Standard

In 2022, the **International Cost Management Standard (ICMS)** released its third edition, incorporating life-cycle carbon into the global cost measurement framework. Now, Bills of Quantities can—and increasingly must—report on both cost and carbon across the entire project lifecycle. This allows for a transparent, apples-to-apples comparison of different design and material options.

ICMS 3 Component	Description
Capital Cost	Traditional construction costs (labor, material, prelims).
Life-Cycle Cost	Costs of energy, maintenance, operations, and refurbishment.
Whole-Life Carbon	**Embodied Carbon** (from materials and supply chain) and **Operational Carbon** (from building use).

14.3 The Business Case—Winning and Saving with Carbon Control

- **Bidding Scorecards:** Many government and private sector tenders now allocate 10-30% of their scoring to proven carbon reduction initiatives.
- **Loan and Investor Covenants:** Access to green bonds and low-interest ESG loans is often linked to quantified carbon goals.
- **Cost and Risk Reduction:** Carbon-saving moves—like modular construction, low-carbon concrete, and local supply chains—often deliver

parallel cost, schedule, and claims reduction benefits.

14.4 Practical Steps: Integrating Carbon Costing

- **Carbon Baselines in BoQ:** Embed carbon as a measured line item for every key element of the project.
- **Construction Stage Tracking:** Use site sensors, supplier declarations, and material passports to measure the actual carbon footprint of delivery, not just the design intent.
- **Whole-Life Modeling:** Implement Life Cycle Assessment (LCA) from the design stage through to operations and demolition.
- **Digital Twins:** Leverage BIM-linked digital twins to simulate and report both actual and forecasted carbon impacts live for clients and regulators.

14.5 Key Takeaways

- Carbon is the new crucial metric, shaping project reputation, bid scores, and financing.
- ICMS 3 and ESG-linked financing are making carbon control a commercial must-have.
- Early, transparent, and digital-first integration of carbon costing is the key to both compliance and strategic advantage.

14.6 Real-Life Applications

1. Launch project "carbon optioneering"

workshops during the pre-tender and early design stages, benchmarking cost and carbon in a single dashboard.

2. Train your QS, estimators, and supply chain teams in carbon cost measurement and reporting, and make it part of their KPIs.
3. Collaborate with your key suppliers to collect and verify Environmental Product Declarations (EPDs) at the procurement and site delivery stages.

Conclusion

Chapter 15

Pulling It All Together—The Resilient Control Model

15.1 From Silos to Systems: Why Integration Matters

Across this book, we've explored how numbers underpin every phase of construction. Yet, in many firms, excellence in one discipline fails to translate into overall project resilience because data, teams, and strategy remain siloed. The world's best builders now operate as learning organizations—connecting every process, person, and lesson into a living, adaptive control model.

15.2 The Resilient Control Model: Anatomy and Approach

This model is a closed feedback loop that links the core pillars discussed throughout this book:

1. **Precision Estimation Pyramid:** Ensures every estimate is layered, evidence-based, and risk-weighted, forming the foundation for a defensible budget.
2. **5-Layer Bid-Win Model:** Embeds intelligence and strategy into every submission, creating "winning by design," not just by price.

3. **Unified Project Controls "Cockpit":** Digitally connects live cost, schedule, risk, procurement, and ESG data into a single source of truth for joint decision-making.
4. **Continuous Learning Loop:** Every project's outcomes—wins, losses, overruns, innovations—are harvested and fed back into the historical index, continuously refining future benchmarks, AI training, and corporate knowledge.

15.3 Leadership and Change Management

Sustainable project resilience is impossible without C-suite sponsorship and organizational humility. This requires:

- **Data Integrity as Strategy:** Data integrity, security, and accessibility must be treated as strategic assets.
- **Cross-functional Training:** Planners learn digital analytics, estimators understand contracts, and commercial teams study risk and ESG.
- **Empowering Feedback:** "Estimate autopsies" and post-mortems must be safe, blameless forums for learning.

15.4 A Glimpse into the Future

The future of project controls will be defined by:

- **AI-Powered Control Rooms:** Real-time digital twins will simulate the cost, schedule, and carbon impacts of every decision before it's made.

- **Global Interoperability:** As standards converge, multinational teams will collaborate seamlessly, benchmarking data and contract frameworks in near real-time.
- **Projects as Products:** Every project will contribute its DNA to a library of reusable, modular intellectual property—scaling innovation in estimation, design, and process.

15.5 Key Takeaways

- Resilience in project controls is no longer just about minimizing overruns but maximizing learning, adaptation, and transparency.
- Integrated models—combining estimation, tendering, controls, digital tools, modularity, and ESG—are the foundation of next-generation construction excellence.
- Leadership must champion not just technical capacity, but a culture of data-driven improvement and ethical stewardship.

15.6 Real-Life Applications

1. Launch a "resilient controls" pilot on a flagship project, applying the best practices from each chapter and benchmarking the outcomes against legacy approaches.
2. Routinely rotate senior staff into digital, data, and controls leadership roles to cascade an integrated mindset across the organization.

Epilogue
The Craftsman's Ledger

When a project ends—when the last scaffold comes down and the noise fades—it's not just the structure that stays behind. What really lingers are the choices we made, the numbers we stood by, and the discipline we held (or didn't) when no one was watching.

An estimate isn't just a number—it's a promise. A dashboard isn't just data—it's a reflection of how we chose to see the truth, early enough to act or late enough to explain. Over the years, I've come to believe that good project control isn't about perfection. It's about being honest with complexity. It's about building in the open, with clarity and intent.

That's what I've tried to share here—a ledger of what I've learned the hard way: on site, under pressure, across teams, and through setbacks. This book isn't meant to sit neatly on a shelf. It's meant to be scribbled in, dog-eared, flagged when things go sideways or when you need to push back with data that speaks for itself.

If a single framework here helps you win a better bid, prevent a late claim, or simply sleep a little easier before that Monday client review (*or Saturday, for those of us in KSA*), then it's done its job.

To everyone involved in shaping projects—whether you're managing takeoffs or overseeing portfolios, reviewing subcontractor claims or presenting to a boardroom—this is your craft. Keep going. Keep asking the harder questions. Keep using numbers not as shields, but as instruments of trust.

Keep building better—by the **Numbers**, for the People.

References

AACE International. *Cost Estimate Classification System (Recommended Practice No. 17R-97).* Morgantown, WV: AACE International.

Arcadis. *Global Construction Disputes Report.* (Annual). Amsterdam: Arcadis.

Autodesk, Inc. *BIM 360 & Revit Documentation.* San Rafael, CA: Autodesk, Inc.

Construction Specifications Institute (CSI). *MasterFormat®.* Alexandria, VA: CSI.

Dubai Municipality & Expo 2020. *Sustainability Reports and Technical Delivery Case Studies.* Dubai, UAE.

Engineering News-Record (ENR). *Global Cost Reports & Productivity Trends.* New York, NY: BNP Media.

FIDIC (International Federation of Consulting Engineers). *Conditions of Contract for Construction (Red Book), Plant and Design-Build (Yellow Book), and EPC/Turnkey Projects (Silver Book).* Geneva, Switzerland: FIDIC.

Indian Roads Congress (IRC). *Manuals on Estimation and Project Delivery.* New Delhi, India: IRC.

International Cost Management Standard (ICMS) Coalition. *ICMS 3: International Construction Measurement Standards – Life Cycle Cost & Carbon.*

International Finance Corporation (IFC). *Green Buildings: A Finance and Policy Blueprint for Emerging Markets.* Washington, D.C.: World Bank Group.

Journal of Construction Engineering and Management. (Peer-reviewed articles). Reston, VA: American Society of Civil Engineers (ASCE).

KPMG. *Smart Construction: How Offsite Manufacturing Can Transform Our Industry.* Amstelveen, Netherlands: KPMG International.

McKinsey & Company. "Reinventing Construction: A Route to Higher Productivity." (Report). McKinsey Global Institute.

McKinsey & Company. "Modular Construction: From Projects to Products." (Report). McKinsey & Company.

Microsoft Corporation. *Microsoft Project Professional User Guide.* Redmond, WA: Microsoft Corporation.

Modular Building Institute. *Best Practices and Case Studies.* Charlottesville, VA: Modular Building

Institute.

NEC. *NEC3/NEC4 Engineering and Construction Contract.* London: Thomas Telford Ltd.

One Click LCA. *Embodied Carbon in Buildings: Calculation Methodology.* Helsinki, Finland: Bionova Ltd.

Oracle Corporation. *Primavera P6 EPPM User Manual.* Austin, TX: Oracle Corporation.

Project Management Institute (PMI). *A Guide to the Project Management Body of Knowledge (PMBOK® Guide), 7th Edition.* Newtown Square, PA: PMI.

PricewaterhouseCoopers (PwC). *Global Construction Disputes Report.* (Annual). London: PwC.

Royal Institution of Chartered Surveyors (RICS). *NRM 1: Order of Cost Estimating and Cost Planning for Capital Building Works; NRM 2: Detailed Measurement for Capital Building Works; NRM 3: Order of Cost Estimating and Cost Planning for Building Maintenance Works.* London: RICS.

Saudi Aramco. *Saudi Aramco Engineering Standards (SAES), Contracting and Cost Management Protocols.* Dhahran, KSA: Saudi Aramco.

Society of Construction Law. *Delay and Disruption Protocol*. UK.

Turner & Townsend. *International Construction Market Survey*. (Annual).

UK Infrastructure and Projects Authority. *The Construction Playbook*. London: The Cabinet Office.

U.S. Bureau of Labor Statistics (BLS). *Producer Price Indexes for Construction Materials*. Washington, D.C.: U.S. Department of Labor.

World Bank. *Life Cycle Costing and Asset Management Guidance*. Washington, D.C.: World Bank Group.

World Economic Forum (WEF). *Shaping the Future of Construction: A Breakthrough in Mindset and Technology*. (Report). Geneva, Switzerland: WEF.

World Green Building Council. *Bringing Embodied Carbon Upfront*. (Report).

Appendix

This section provides supplementary materials, including a glossary of key industry terms, detailed schedule breakdowns, and practical checklists mentioned throughout the book.

Appendix A: Glossary of Key Terms and Acronyms

- **AACEI (Association for the Advancement of Cost Engineering International):** An organization focused on total cost management, rigorous cost estimation, risk, and forensic analysis.
- **BIM (Building Information Modeling):** A digital representation of a facility. 5D BIM links the 3D model with time (4D) and cost (5D).
- **BoQ (Bill of Quantities):** A document that provides itemized measurements of materials and labor required for a construction project.
- **CDE (Common Data Environment):** A single source of information for a project, used to collect, manage, and share information among all team members.

- **CSI MasterFormat:** A standard for organizing specifications and other written information for commercial and institutional building projects in the U.S. and Canada.
- **EVM (Earned Value Management):** A project management technique for measuring project performance and progress in an objective manner.
- **FAC (Final Acceptance Certificate):** The final milestone confirming all contractual obligations have been met.
- **FAT (Factory Acceptance Test):** An inspection conducted to verify that equipment meets its specifications before being shipped to the site.
- **FEED (Front-End Engineering Design):** An engineering phase where the scope is firmly defined to a level sufficient for EPC tendering.
- **FIDIC (International Federation of Consulting Engineers):** An international standards organization for the construction industry, best known for its suite of contract conditions.
- **IFC (Issued for Construction):** The status of an engineering drawing that is finalized and

approved for use in construction.

- **LLI (Long-Lead Item):** A critical piece of equipment or material with a long delivery time that is often on the project's critical path.
- **MCC (Mechanical Completion Certificate):** A formal certificate indicating that the facility is built to specification and ready for commissioning.
- **MIJ (Monolithic Isolation Joint):** A specialized component used to electrically isolate sections of a pipeline for corrosion control.
- **NMR (Non-Material Requisition):** A requisition used for specialized engineering materials that are not standard bulk items, such as instruments or special pipeline components.
- **PAC (Provisional Acceptance Certificate):** A certificate issued after successful startup that signifies the beginning of the warranty period.
- **P&ID (Piping and Instrumentation Diagram):** A detailed diagram in the process industry which shows the piping and vessels in the process flow, together with the

instrumentation and control devices.

- **PMBOK (Project Management Body of Knowledge):** A guide published by PMI that documents standards and best practices for project management.
- **PMP (Project Management Professional):** A globally recognized professional certification in project management offered by PMI.
- **PO (Purchase Order):** A commercial document issued by a buyer to a seller, indicating types, quantities, and agreed prices for products or services.
- **RICS (Royal Institution of Chartered Surveyors):** A professional body that accredits professionals within the land, property, construction, and infrastructure sectors worldwide. Known for the New Rules of Measurement (NRM).
- **ROW (Right of Way):** The legal right, established by usage or grant, to pass along a specific route through grounds or property belonging to another.
- **RTU (Remote Terminal Unit):** A field computer that sends pipeline data back to the central control room.

- **WBS (Work Breakdown Structure):** A deliverable-oriented breakdown of a project into smaller components.

Appendix B: Sample Level IV WBS for a Pipeline Project

The following is a representative extract from a Level IV Work Breakdown Structure (WBS) for a pipeline project, forming the basis for detailed reporting and invoicing.

- **1.0 Project Management**
    - 1.1 Project Controls & Reporting
        - 1.1.2 Cost Management & Invoicing
            - 1.1.2.1 Submit Monthly Progress Invoice to Aramco
- **2.0 Engineering**
    - 2.2 Process Engineering
        - 2.2.1 P&ID Development
            - 2.2.1.3 Issue P&IDs Issued for Construction (IFC)
    - 2.4 Mechanical Engineering
        - 2.4.1 Pig Launcher/Receiver Engineering
            - 2.4.1.3 Vendor Drawing Review & Approval
- **3.0 Procurement**
    - 3.2 Long-Lead Items (LLI) - Mainline Valves

        - 3.2.1.2 Award Purchase Order (PO)
        - 3.2.1.4 Deliver Mainline Valves to Site
    - 3.3 Bulk Materials - Line Pipe
        - 3.3.1.3 Deliver Line Pipe to Site - Lot 1
- **4.0 Construction**
    - 4.2 Right of Way (ROW)
        - 4.2.1.2 Clear & Grade ROW
    - 4.3 Pipeline Installation
        - 4.3.2 Mainline Welding
    - 4.5 Tie-Ins
        - 4.5.1 Mainline Section Tie-In Welds (Golden Welds)
- **5.0 Pre-commissioning & Commissioning**
    - 5.1 Pre-commissioning Activities
        - 5.1.1 Pipeline Section 1 Hydrotest
    - 5.2 Commissioning & Startup
        - 5.2.2.2 Introduce Hydrocarbons (First Gas/Oil)
- **6.0 Project Closeout**
    - 6.1 Final Documentation
        - 6.1.1.3 Submit Final Dossier to Aramco

Appendix C: Sample Estimate Autopsy Checklist

This checklist is designed to guide a structured post-project session to review estimate accuracy, analyze deviations, and institutionalize lessons learned.

- **Project Details**
    - Project Name & ID:
    - Date of Review:
    - Attendees & Roles:
- **Estimate Performance Review**
    - What was the final cost deviation from the baseline estimate?
    - What was the final schedule deviation?
    - Which were the top 3 areas with the largest cost overruns?
    - Which were the top 3 areas with the largest cost underruns?
- **Root Cause Analysis**
    - **Scope:** Were there significant changes

from the original WBS? Were scope definitions clear?

- **Quantities:** Were there major errors in the initial take-offs? How did BIM/Digital Take-Offs perform versus manual checks?
- **Rates:** Were labor, material, or equipment rates benchmarked correctly? Which rates were most volatile?
- **Productivity:** Did actual field productivity match the assumptions in the estimate?
- **Risk & Contingency:** Was the original contingency adequate? Which unforeseen risks materialized? Was contingency tracked and managed actively?

- **Lessons Learned & Actions**
  - What specific benchmarks in our historical database need to be updated (e.g., cost per ton of steel, productivity norms for welding)?
  - What changes should be made to our

estimation process or tools?

- Who is the "Estimation Champion" responsible for implementing these changes?
- Date for next review:

Praise for *Numbers That Build*

Mr. Juan Carlos - Operations Manager, Madrid, Spain

"Finally, a book that speaks the language of high-stakes project delivery in our region. Tauheed Jan doesn't just give you formulas; he gives you strategy. His 5-Layer Bid-Win Model is a game-changer, but it was his frank discussion on managing the 'politics of change' that really hit home. This is more than a book; it's a playbook for anyone serious about building a profitable and resilient construction business in the modern world. An essential and deeply insightful read."

Mr. Ajay Pandit Patil - Estimation Manager, Al Khobar, Kingdom of Saudi Arabia

"A masterclass in the art and science of estimation. In a field where we are often pressured to 'sharpen the pencil,' Tauheed provides a structured, defensible methodology with his Precision Estimation Pyramid. I found the chapter breaking down the nuances between international rulebooks like FIDIC and RICS particularly valuable for our multinational JVs. This is an indispensable guide that will sit on my desk for daily reference, not on a shelf gathering dust."

Mr. Muzaffar Sikandar - Project Controls Manager, KSA

"Tauheed doesn't just rehash old principles; he tackles the future head-on. This book is a rare bridge between traditional project controls and the disruptive forces reshaping our industry. The chapters on leveraging AI for forecasting, the commercial implications of modular construction, and the critical need for ESG costing are incredibly timely.

Numbers That Build provides a strategic roadmap for navigating the volatility and complexity that now define our work. Highly recommended for any leader looking to build a competitive edge."

Mr. Ranjit Nair - Project Director, KSA

"This is the book I wish I had when I started my career. The deep dive into the EPC controls model, especially the breakdown of engineering deliverables and the procurement lifecycle, is the most practical guide I have ever read. Tauheed demystifies complex client requirements and provides a clear link between a schedule activity in Primavera P6 and the final invoice. For any project controls professional working on major projects, this book is like having a seasoned mentor guiding you through every step. Its clarity and field-tested wisdom are unmatched

www.ingramcontent.com/pod-product-compliance
Lightning Source LLC
Chambersburg PA
CBHW050020170726
48282CB00025B/479
* 9 7 8 9 3 3 4 3 7 1 7 5 8 *